The Christian Adventure

Beginning the Exciting Journey of Faith

S T E P   1

Bill Bright

NewLife
PUBLICATIONS
A MINISTRY OF CAMPUS CRUSADE FOR CHRIST

Ten Basic Steps Toward Christian Maturity
Step 1: The Christian Adventure

Published by
NewLife Publications
100 Lake Hart Drive
Orlando, FL 32832-0100

Printed in the United States of America.

ISBN: 1-56399-030-X

Thomas Nelson Inc., Nashville, Tennessee, is the exclusive distributor of this book to the trade markets in the United States and the District of Columbia.

Distributed in Canada by Campus Crusade for Christ of Canada, Surrey, B.C.

Unless otherwise indicated, all Scripture references are from the *New International Version*, © 1973, 1978, 1984 by the International Bible Society. Published by Zondervan Bible Publishers, Grand Rapids, Michigan.

Scripture quotations designated TLB are from *The Living Bible*, © 1971 by Tyndale House Publishers, Wheaton, Illinois.

Any royalties from this book or the many other books by Bill Bright are dedicated to the glory of God and designated to the various ministries of Campus Crusade for Christ/*NewLife2000*.

For more information, write:

L.I.F.E.—P. O. Box 40, Flemmington Markets, 2129, Australia
Campus Crusade for Christ of Canada—Box 300, Vancouver, B.C., V6C 2X3, Canada
Campus Crusade for Christ—Fairgate House, King's Road, Tyseley, Birmingham, B11 2AA, England
Lay Institute for Evangelism—P. O. Box 8786, Auckland 3, New Zealand
Campus Crusade for Christ—Alexandra, P. O. Box 0205, Singapore 9115, Singapore
Great Commission Movement of Nigeria—P. O. Box 500, Jos, Plateau State Nigeria, West Africa
Campus Crusade for Christ International—100 Sunport Lane, Orlando, FL 32809, USA

Contents

Acknowledgments 4

A Personal Word 5

What This Study Will Do for You 7

How to Use This Study 9

Why All the Excitement? 12

LESSONS

    1 ❖ The Christian's Certainty 15

    2 ❖ The Christ-Controlled Life 21

    3 ❖ Five Principles of Growth 31

    4 ❖ The Christian's Authority 43

    5 ❖ Learning to Pray 51

    6 ❖ The Importance of the Church 57

    7 ❖ Recap 65

Keys to Dynamic Living 71

Resources to Help You Grow in Christ 73

Acknowledgments

The *Ten Basic Steps Toward Christian Maturity* series was a product of necessity. As the ministry of Campus Crusade for Christ expanded rapidly to scores of campuses across America, thousands of students committed their lives to Christ—several hundred on a single campus. Individual follow-up of all new converts soon became impossible. Who was to help them grow in their new-found faith?

A Bible study series designed for new Christians was desperately needed—a study that would stimulate individuals and groups to explore the depths and the riches of God's Word. Although several excellent studies were available, we felt the particular need of new material for these college students.

In 1955, I asked several of my fellow staff associates to assist me in the preparation of Bible studies that would stimulate both evangelism and Christian growth in a new believer. The contribution by campus staff members was especially significant because of their constant contact with students in introducing them to Christ and meeting regularly with them to disciple them. Thus, the *Ten Basic Steps Toward Christian Maturity* was the fruit of our combined labor.

Since that modest beginning, many other members of the staff have contributed generously. On occasion, for example, I found myself involved in research and writing sessions with several of our staff, all seminary graduates, some with advanced degrees and one with his doctorate in theology. More important, all were actively engaged in "winning, building, and sending men" for Christ.

For this latest edition, I want to thank Don Tanner for his professional assistance in revising, expanding, and editing the contents. I also want to thank Joette Whims and Jean Bryant for their extensive help and for joining Don and me in the editorial process.

A Personal Word

Drew was a sharp, dedicated high school senior who provided leadership to the youth group in his church. Through the influence of his parents and a good church, he received Christ as a young boy. But like many young people growing up in church, he experienced little spiritual growth.

One summer Drew rededicated his life to Christ, but he still felt something was missing. Today, however, that has changed. His discovery of the person and power of God's Holy Spirit has transformed him into a joyful Christian and a vibrant witness for Christ.

Drew came to realize that living the Christian life is not simply difficult—it is impossible. Only through the power of the Holy Spirit within us can we possibly have the strength to resist temptation and make the right choices.

"The message had never reached me that I must let the Lord, in the form of the Holy Spirit, live the Christian life through me," Drew says. "I cannot express the joy I felt when I discovered that the 'burden' of living the Christian life is really no burden at all because the Holy Spirit will live it through me if I invite Him and trust Him to do so."

The Christian life is a great adventure because God loves us and has a wonderful, exciting plan for us. We are not creatures of chance, brought into the world for a meaningless, miserable existence; rather, we are people of destiny, created for meaningful, fruitful, and joyful lives.

If you would like to discover this power source for your life and ministry, take my hand and come with me. In this study we are going on an exciting journey through many important scriptural concepts. I want to share with you vital truths that will help you understand and experience the great adventure of the Christian life.

I guarantee that, as you apply what you learn in this book to your daily living, your life will never be the same.

The spiritual wildernesses of your life will diminish in size and frequency. You will learn how to delight in the Lord every day—even when your circumstances are not always delightful. Boredom will become excitement. Hopelessness will become hope. Your walk with God will take on a new dimension of purpose and power because you are allowing the Holy Spirit to do His work in and through your life.

My prayer is that this study will bless and enrich your life in a dramatic, supernatural way, that you will find encouragement in your growth toward full maturity in Jesus Christ as you become more like Him, and that you will become more effective in your personal witness for Him.

What This Study Will Do for You

A medical doctor approached me with great excitement at the conclusion of a Campus Crusade for Christ training conference. He was overflowing with joy and excitement.

"Since I have learned how to be filled with the Holy Spirit and walk in His power, the Christian life has become a great adventure for me!" he exclaimed. "Now, I want everyone to experience this same adventure with Christ."

This study is designed to help you know how to enjoy what this man and millions of other Christians around the world have experienced: the adventure of a full, abundant, purposeful, and fruitful life in Christ. If you have been living in spiritual defeat—powerless and fruitless, wondering if there is any validity to the Christian life—you will find hope in these pages.

You will discover what it really means to follow Jesus Christ as Lord and Master and where the church fits into your life. You will learn the five principles of personal growth as a Christian. And you will see how the indwelling life of Christ is the key to experiencing a victorious Christian life.

Certain basic spiritual truths, when understood and experienced by faith, bring revolutionary spiritual benefits. The proven

You will discover what it really means to follow Jesus Christ as Lord and Master.

7

principles you are about to study can help you be more consistent in your walk with God and be more effective in your witness for our dear Savior.

I assure you that if you apply the proven concepts presented in this study, you will discover a life truly without equal.

Foundation for Faith

Step 1: The Christian Adventure is part of the *Ten Basic Steps Toward Christian Maturity*, a time-tested study series designed to provide you with a sure foundation for your faith. Hundreds of thousands have benefited from this Bible study series during the almost forty years since it was first published in its original form.

When you complete Step 1, I encourage you to continue your study with the rest of the Steps.

If you are a new Christian, the *Ten Basic Steps* will acquaint you with the major doctrines of the Christian faith. By applying the principles you will learn, you will grow spiritually and find solutions to problems you are likely to face as a new believer.

If you are a mature Christian, you will discover the tools you need to help others receive Christ and grow in their faith. Your own commitment to our Lord will be affirmed, and you will discover how to develop an effective devotional and study plan.

The series includes an individual booklet for the introductory study and one for each of the ten Steps. These study guides correlate with the expanded and updated *Handbook for Christian Maturity* and *Ten Basic Steps Leader's Guide*.

Each Step reveals a different facet of the Christian life and truth, and each contains lessons for study that can be used during your personal quiet time or in a group setting.

I encourage you to pursue the study of Step 1 with an open, eager mind. As you read, continually pray that God will show you how to relate the principles you learn to your own situation. Begin to apply them on a daily basis, and you will keep the energy and joy alive in your walk with God as you experience the Christian adventure.

How to Use This Study

On page 12 of this Step, you will find the preparatory article, "Why All the Excitement?" The article will give you a clear perspective on the exciting adventure of Christian living. Read it carefully before you begin Lesson 1. Review it prayerfully during your study.

This Step contains six lessons plus a "Recap" or review. Each lesson is divided into two sections: the Bible Study and the Life Application. Begin by noting the Objective for the lesson you are studying. The Objective states the main goal for your study. Keep it in mind as you continue through the lesson.

Take time to memorize the referenced Scripture verses. Learn each verse by writing it on a small card to carry with you. You can buy cards for these verses at any bookstore or print shop, or you can make your own by using filing cards. Review daily the verses you have memorized.

Our Lord has commanded that we learn His Word. Proverbs 7:1–3 reminds us:

> My son, keep my words and store up my commands within you. Keep my commands and you will live; guard my teachings as the apple of your eye. Bind them on your fingers; write them on the tablet of your heart.

Your most important objective in your study is to meet with God in a loving, personal way.

As you meditate on the verses you have memorized and claim God's promises, you will experience the joy, victory, and power that God's Word gives to your Christian walk. When you have finished all the studies in the entire series, you will be able to develop your own Bible study, continuing to use a systematic method for memorizing God's Word.

How to Study the Lessons

Casual Bible reading uncovers valuable spiritual facts that lie near the surface. But understanding the deeper truths requires study. Often the difference between reading and studying is a pen and notepad.

Every lesson in this study covers an important topic and gives you an opportunity to record your answers to the questions. Plan to spend a minimum of thirty minutes each day—preferably in the morning—in Bible study, meditation, and prayer.

Remember, the most important objective and benefit of a quiet time or Bible study is not to acquire knowledge or accumulate biblical information but to meet with God in a loving, personal way.

Here are some suggestions to help you in your study time:

◆ Plan a specific time and place to work on these studies. Make an appointment with God; then keep it.

◆ Use a pen or pencil, your Bible, and this booklet.

◆ Begin with prayer for God's presence, blessing, and wisdom.

◆ Meditate on the Objective to determine how it fits into your circumstances.

◆ Memorize the suggested verses.

◆ Proceed to the Bible study, trusting God to use it to teach you. Prayerfully anticipate His presence with you. Work carefully, reading the Scripture passages and thinking through the questions. Answer each as completely as possible.

◆ When you come to the Life Application, answer the questions honestly and begin to apply them to your own life.

◆ Prayerfully read through the lesson again and reevaluate your Life Application answers. Do they need changing? Or adjusting?

◆ Review the memory verses.

◆ Consider the Objective again and determine if it has been accomplished. If not, what do you need to do?

◆ Close with a prayer of thanksgiving, and ask God to help you grow spiritually in the areas He has specifically revealed to you.

◆ When you complete the first six lessons of this Step, spend extra time on the Recap to make sure you understand every lesson thoroughly.

◆ If you need more study of this Step, ask God for wisdom again and go through whatever lesson(s) you need to review, repeating the process until you do understand and are able to apply the truths to your own life.

These studies are not intended as a complete development of Christian beliefs. However, a careful study of the material will give you, with God's help, a sufficient understanding of how you can know and apply God's plan for your life. The spiritual truths contained here will help you meet with our Lord Jesus Christ in an intimate way and discover the full and abundant life that Jesus promised (John 10:10).

Do not rush through the lessons. Take plenty of time to think through the questions. Meditate on them. Absorb the truths presented, and make the application a part of your life. Give God a chance to speak to you, and let the Holy Spirit teach you. As you spend time with our Lord in prayer and study, and as you trust and obey Him, you will experience the amazing joy of His presence (John 14:21).

Why All the Excitement?

Jesus Christ is the most remarkable and fascinating person in history. He has inspired more hope, taught more compassion, and shown more love than any other man who has ever lived.

When He walked on earth, Jesus stirred people wherever He went. Crowds followed Him; hands reached out to Him; voices called to Him; people pushed and sometimes trampled one another just to see Him, to hear Him teach, to bring their sick to be healed.

Jesus' popularity grew until many wanted to make Him king of the Jews. Once, when He entered Jerusalem, the capital city of Israel, crowds lining the wayside pulled off their cloaks and broke off palm branches to throw in front of Him. Voices shouted:

"Hosanna to the Son of David!"

"Blessed is He who comes in the name of the Lord!"

"Hosanna in the highest!"

When he entered Jerusalem, the whole city took notice.

People gathered asking, "Who is this man?"

Others answered, "This is Jesus, the prophet from Nazareth" (Matthew 21:9–11).

To know Jesus Christ personally as Savior and Lord is the greatest privilege and adventure that we can ever experience.

What was there about this man that caused a stir wherever He went? Down through the centuries, countless millions of people have considered the historical person of Jesus of Nazareth. Today men and women everywhere are excited about Him.

Millions Hunger for Christ

My wife, Vonette, and I, along with more than forty thousand of our dedicated full-time staff, associate staff, and trained volunteers, have observed a hunger for Jesus in approximately two hundred countries. On university campuses, in hundreds of metropolitan centers, in towns, villages, and primitive or remote areas, we have witnessed this hunger for Christ as we have shared the "most wonderful news ever announced" with hundreds of millions.

Perhaps you are wondering, *What's all the excitement? Why do His life and teachings still generate such interest today?*

Indeed, there has never been anyone who could compare with Jesus of Nazareth. Philip Schaff, well-known historian and author of *The History of the Christian Church,* said:

> Jesus of Nazareth, without money and arms, conquered more millions than Alexander, Caesar, Mohammed and Napoleon; without science and learning, He shed more light on things human and divine than all the philosophers and scholars combined; without the eloquence of the school, He spoke words of life such as were never spoken before, nor since, and produced effects which lie beyond the reach of orator or poet.
>
> Without writing a single line, He has set more pens in motion and furnished themes for more sermons, orations, discussions, works of art, learned volumes, and sweet songs of praise than the whole army of great men of ancient and modern times.
>
> Born in a manger and crucified as a malefactor, He now controls the destinies of the civilized world and rules a spiritual empire which embraces one-third of the inhabitants of the globe.[1]

[1] Philip Schaff, *The Person of Christ* (New York: American Tract Society, 1913), p.33.

Indeed, without fear of contradiction, we can regard Jesus Christ as history's greatest revolutionary. Everything about Him was unique: the prophecies of His coming. His birth. His life. His teachings. His miracles. His death. His resurrection. His influence on history and in the lives of hundreds of millions of people.

What does all this mean to us today? The Bible tells us:

> Christ is the exact likeness of the unseen God. He existed before God made anything at all, and, in fact, Christ himself is the Creator who made everything in heaven and earth, the things we can see and the things we can't…He was before all else began and it is his power that holds everything together (Colossians 1:15–17, TLB).

His creation includes you. Since we are created by Jesus Christ, He alone holds the answer to the basic questions of life: *Who am I? Where did I come from? Why am I here? Where am I going?*

Experiencing True Purpose

If you have trusted Him, He has taken up residence in your life. As you yield complete control to Him, inviting Him to be the Lord of every area of your being, you will discover the answers to these questions; you will experience the true purpose for which He created you.

In exchange for a life of defeat and frustration, Christ will give you His victory, His power.

Many people believe Christianity must be patiently endured in anticipation of heaven. But our Lord did not intend it to be this way. He meant for your Christian life to be joyful, fruitful, and exciting. To know Jesus Christ personally as Savior and Lord is the greatest privilege and adventure that we can ever experience.

Delivered from the tyranny of sin, liberated from the "darkness and gloom of Satan's kingdom" and having been brought "into the Kingdom of His [God's] dear Son" (Colossians 1:13,14, TLB), we have true purpose for living. Indeed, the secret to a joyful and fulfilling life is the purpose you find in Jesus. He alone can give you unshakable peace in a world of turmoil, and inexhaustible power for daily living.

The Christian's Certainty

Believers of Old Testament times looked forward to the coming of their Messiah. New Testament believers look back to the cross and the resurrection. Both of these events culminate in the unique person of Jesus Christ.

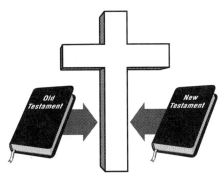

Objective: To give the new Christian assurance of eternal life and of Christ's presence in his life

Read: John 3:1–20 and 1 John 5:9–15

Memorize: 1 John 5:13

The apostle Paul says, "It was through what His Son did that God cleared a path for everything to come to Him—all things in heaven and on earth—for Christ's death on the cross has made peace with God for all by His blood...and now as a result Christ has brought you into the very presence of God, and you are standing there before Him with nothing left against you...the only condition is that you fully believe the Truth, standing in it steadfast and firm, strong in the Lord, convinced of the Good News that Jesus died

15

for you, and never shifting from trusting Him to save you" (Colossians 1:20–23, TLB).

Hundreds of millions of people around the world have discovered this marvelous "path" because of Jesus' death on the cross and His bodily resurrection from the dead.

Jesus' death bridged the gulf between the holiness of God and the sinfulness of man. He died to pay the penalty of our sin and rescue us "out of the darkness and gloom of Satan's kingdom" and bring us "into the Kingdom of His dear Son, who bought our freedom with His blood and forgave us all our sins" (Colossians 1:13,14, TLB). But without His resurrection and ascension, His sacrifice would have been incomplete, and we would have remained under the penalty of death (1 Corinthians 15:17).

To believe in Jesus Christ as the Savior of the world is to believe in a living person. People often ask, "What is the meaning of belief?" *The Amplified New Testament* expresses the full meaning of the term *believe* as "adhere to, trust in, and rely on." The Gospel of John has been called the Gospel of Belief. The word *believe* occurs many times in the book of John. Chapter 20, verse 31, expresses the purpose of that book:

> These are written that you may believe that Jesus is the Christ, the Son of God, and that by believing you may have life in His name.

The living Savior, therefore, is the basis for Christian confidence. The resurrection is the foundation of our certainty that we have eternal life in Christ and that we experience daily the indwelling presence of our living Savior.

❖
Bible Study

Christian Certainty

1. What must one do to become a Christian (John 1:12)?

Receive and believe

2. To be a son of God is to be born of whom (John 1:13)?

Born of God.

3. To believe in Jesus Christ is to possess and to be free from what (John 5:24)?

4. What did Christ do with our sins (1 Peter 2:24,25)?

Based our Sins

How should this affect our lives?

5. What three things characterize Jesus' sheep (John 10:27)?

1) *Hear my Voice*
2) *Know me.*
3) *follow me*

6. What is your relationship with Christ, as He Himself states in John 10:18–30?

7. What are the implications of failing to believe the testimony that God has given regarding His Son (1 John 5:10,11)?

8. The resurrection of Jesus is history's most revolutionary event. How does it prove Christ's claim to be God (Romans 1:4)?

Why is the resurrection so essential to our faith (1 Corinthians 15:17; Ephesians 2:4–10)?

New Life

1. In John 3:3–7 what did Jesus tell Nicodemus about seeing and entering the kingdom of God?

2. At physical birth one receives many things he is not aware of: family name, privileges, wealth, love, care, and protection. At spiritual birth one becomes a son of God and receives eternal life, a divine inheritance, and God's love, care, and protection. God has given us these because of His great love. God's gifts are never based on man's changing emotions, but on His own unchanging Word.

In your own words describe what you have, according to these verses:

Ephesians 1:7

Romans 5:1

Romans 3:22

Colossians 1:27

3. As you begin to live the Christian life, what three
evidences in your life will assure you that you know
Jesus Christ?
1 John 2:3

1 John 3:14

Romans 8:16

LIFE APPLICATION

1 Who is Jesus Christ to you?

2 What is your relationship with God?

3 What kind of life do you now possess?

4 What about your sins?

5 Why are you sure (or doubtful) of your salvation?

6 What changes do you believe have taken place because Christ is in your life?

❖ ❖ ❖

The Christ-Controlled Life

There is a throne, a control center—the intersection of one's intellect, emotions, and will—in every life. Either self or Christ is on that throne. Let me illustrate.

I like to plan as far in advance as possible, especially for key events. But occasionally I get so busy with the many details of our worldwide ministry that an important item slips through.

With a key conference only a couple of weeks away, I had just realized the need for a set of printed materials that would be of tremendous benefit to the attendees.

As I shared the urgency with the department director responsible for this need, he responded, "Bill, we're full up already. Two weeks just isn't enough time."

I became impatient. Couldn't my associate see that we are in a war for men's souls, that we must seize opportunities when they arise and not limit our efforts to 8-to-5 workdays? I made my point clear to him.

"But if we had more notice…," he protested. "There just is no way we can squeeze

Objective: To show how the indwelling Christ is the key to the Christian life

Read: 1 Corinthians 2:11; 3:5; Galatians 5:16–24

Memorize: Philippians 4:13

in such a huge job with so little time. There's the writing, then the design, typesetting, and artwork, then the printing..."

It seemed obvious that he did not share my burden for the upcoming event. I pressed my point. "Look, this is an important international conference," I said firmly, my voice rising. "And this is no time for 'business as usual.' Please find a way to finish this project in time for the conference, even if you have to work around the clock."

I could tell that my colleague was frustrated. But I reasoned, *We need those printed materials. Whatever it takes, we need them.*

Within a few moments after our conversation, I sensed the conviction of the Holy Spirit. Yes, even in our well-intended service of the Lord, we can stumble—and in the name of godliness I had offended a dear brother in Christ. I had failed to give him and his staff the benefit of the doubt—failed to take into account the tough workload they already were facing each day.

Instead of asking him to think through the possibilities with me and helping him rearrange his priorities to accommodate the new task, I had virtually ordered him to get the project done and shown little appreciation for the many late evenings his team was already devoting to their work. I had reacted impatiently rather than in a spirit of love, understanding, and teamwork.

At this point I had a choice to make.

On the one hand, I could let it go. After all, doesn't the head of a large organization have the right to ramrod projects through when necessary? Didn't the end (the strategic international conference) justify the means (get the job done no matter what it takes)? And didn't my associate's hesitant attitude warrant a stern talking-to about the urgency of the hour?

By all human standards, I probably could have justified letting the incident go. But deep inside I would have been restless and uncomfortable as the Holy Spirit continued to point out my sin to me, and God would not have blessed my efforts on His behalf as long as this sin remained unconfessed. On top of that, several of my dear co-workers would have continued to hurt as a result of my callous attitude.

On the other hand, I could deal with the problem by taking scriptural action to clear the slate. The unrest in my conscience was the Holy Spirit cross-examining me as I tried to rationalize my behavior. What I had thought was forceful leadership, He was identifying as the sins of impatience and unjustifiable anger.

I knew that taking scriptural action was the only choice I could make that would please my Lord. I confessed my sin to Him and appropriated His forgiveness.

Then came the toughest part.

I drove down to the office complex where my associate and his team were located and asked their forgiveness. We cried and laughed and prayed together, sensing a fresh outpouring of God's love in our midst. Then we talked through our mutual needs and found a way—as teammates—to rearrange priorities and accomplish the task—on time!

That is what the Christian life is all about—just keeping Christ on the throne. You do this when you understand how to walk in the control and power of the Holy Spirit, for the Holy Spirit came for the express purpose of glorifying Christ by enabling the believer to live a holy life and to be a fruitful witness for our dear Savior.

Many people have misconceptions about the Christian life. Some argue that once they have received Jesus Christ into their lives by faith, it is up to them to live a life pleasing to God in their own strength. Others believe that Christ has entered their lives to help them live and work for God's glory. These ideas of Christian living look good on the surface, but each contains a weakness that actually undermines the basis of vital Christian living.

In light of Romans 7:18, Galatians 2:20, and Romans 1:17, what do you think the basic approach should be? Write your answer here:

Someone said, "the Christian life is not difficult—it is impossible." Only one person has ever lived the Christian life, and that was Jesus Christ. Today He desires to go on living His life through

Christians whom He indwells. J. B. Phillips, in the preface (p. xiv) to his translation of a portion of the New Testament, *Letters to Young Churches,* said:

> The great difference between present-day Christianity and that of which we read in these letters is that to us it is primarily a performance, while to them it was a real experience. We are apt to reduce the Christian religion to a code, or at best a rule of heart and life. To those men it is quite plainly the invasion of their lives by a new quality of life altogether. They do not hesitate to describe this as Christ "living in" them.

Before His death, Christ told His disciples that it was best for Him to leave them so that the Spirit of God might come to dwell in each of them (John 14:16–20; 16:7). In other words, Christ was physically departing from His disciples so that He might always be present spiritually within each of them.

Today when a person places his faith in Christ, Christ comes to dwell within him by means of the Holy Spirit (Romans 8:9). His purpose for dwelling in us is that He might live His life through us. Many Christians are trying to operate on their own finite ability instead of Christ's infinite power.

Have you ever asked yourself, *How can I experience the victorious life of Christ?*[1] To find the answer, let's examine the three types of persons in the world today: the non-Christian (natural man), the spiritual Christian, and the worldly or carnal Christian.

❖

Bible Study

The Non-Christian or Natural Man

In the following diagram, this circle represents the life of the person who has never received Christ as Savior and Lord. Christ stands outside the door of the life, seeking entrance (Revelation 3:20).

---

[1] For additional information on how you can experience the victorious life, see *Keys to Dynamic Living*, p. 71.

Self-Directed Life

S – Self is on the throne

✝ – Christ is outside the life

● – Interests are directed by
self, often resulting in
discord and frustration

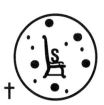

1. What adjective do you think best describes the man who
does not understand the things of the Spirit of God
(1 Corinthians 2:14)? *Foolish man*

2. What terms describe self in the following verses?

Romans 6:6

old self is crucified
old sin is destroyed.

Galatians 5:16,17

Believers walk, Walk in the spirit
don't let your flesh work contrary to the spirit

3. List at least three characteristics of the man without Christ,
as described in Ephesians 2:1–3.

1) *dead and in trespasses and sins*

2) *disobedience*

3) *lust of our flesh*

4. What is the condition of the heart of the natural man
(Jeremiah 17:9)?

The heart deceitful above all things

5. List the thirteen sins that Jesus said come from the heart
of man (Mark 7:20–23).

evil thoughts, adulteries, fornications,
murders, thefts, covetousness, wickedness
deceit, lasciviousness, evil eye, blasphemy, pride
foolishness, (sex lose)

6. Summarize the relationship between God and the non-Christian (John 3:36).

not see life. but the wrath of God abideth on him.

7. How, then, does one become a Christian (John 1:12; Revelation 3:20)?

receive him. power to become the sons of God.

The Spiritual or Christ-Controlled Christian

This circle represents the life of the person who has invited Jesus Christ to come into his life and who is allowing Him to control and empower his life. Christ is occupying His rightful place on the throne of the life. Self has been dethroned.

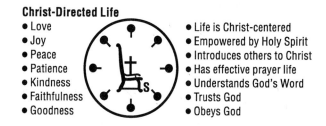

Christ-Directed Life
- Love
- Joy
- Peace
- Patience
- Kindness
- Faithfulness
- Goodness

- Life is Christ-centered
- Empowered by Holy Spirit
- Introduces others to Christ
- Has effective prayer life
- Understands God's Word
- Trusts God
- Obeys God

1. What are some other characteristics of a life controlled by God's Spirit (Galatians 5:22,23)?

Meekness, temperance, gentleness

2. In what sense could the Spirit-controlled life be called the exchanged life (Galatians 2:20)? *old life is crucified.*

3. Where does the Christian receive the power to live this otherwise impossible life (Philippians 4:13)? *Through the power of Christ*

4. What does the spiritual Christian have that will enable him to understand the things of God (1 Corinthians 2:14–16)? *Spirit of God*

The Worldly Christian and the Solution

In 1 Corinthians 3:1–3, the apostle Paul addresses the Christians as "worldly" ["carnal," King James Version] (self-centered), rather than spiritual (Christ-centered). The following diagram represents a life in which the person's ego has asserted itself. Self has usurped the throne of the life, and Christ has stepped down. The result is the loss of the individual's fellowship with God though he is still a Christian.

Self-Directed Life
- Legalistic attitude
- Impure thoughts
- Jealousy
- Guilt
- Worry
- Discouragement
- Critical spirit
- Frustration
- Aimlessness
- Fear

- Ignorance of his spiritual heritage
- Unbelief
- Disobedience
- Loss of love for God and for others
- Poor prayer life
- No desire for Bible study

1. Describe the worldly Christian as presented in 1 Corinthians 3:1–3. *you get feed milk not meat, you are babes.*

Name five or six practices that result from worldliness
(Galatians 5:19–21). *adultery, fornication,
uncleanness, lasciviousness, witchcraft
hatred.*

Summarize in your own words the relationship between the
worldly mind and God, as described in Romans 8:7.

rebellish spirit.

2. The solution to worldliness (the self-controlled life) is
   threefold:

   1) We must *confess* our sins, recognizing that we have been
      rulers of our own lives. When we confess them, what will
      God do (1 John 1:9)?

      *- faithful and just to forgive us
      our sins.*

      Read Proverbs 28:13. What is the result of not
      admitting sin?

      you shall not prosper

      What is the result of admitting sin (Proverbs 28:13;
      Psalm 32:1)? *Bless if you admit sins*

   2) We must *surrender,* or yield, the throne to Christ. State
      in your own words how Paul describes the act of present-
      ing ourselves to God in Romans 12:1,2.

      *present your Body as a living
      sacrifice, be transformed by
      the renewing of your mind.*

3) By *faith* we must *recognize* that Christ assumed control of our lives upon our invitation. How can you be sure that if you ask Jesus Christ to assume His rightful place on the throne of your life, He will do so (1 John 5:14,15)?

whatever you ask

We receive the Lord Jesus Christ by faith. How then do we allow Him to control our lives moment by moment (Colossians 2:6)?

received Christ Walk ye in him

Give three reasons faith is so important (Hebrews 11:6; Romans 14:23; Romans 1:17).

1) *without faith*

2) *no faith is sin*

3) *righteous live by faith.*

L I F E   A P P L I C A T I O N

The secret of the abundant life is to allow Jesus Christ to control your life moment by moment through His Holy Spirit living within you. When you realize that you have sinned, confess your sin immediately; thank God for forgiving you and continue to walk in fellowship with God.

1 In prayer, examine your attitude. Do you honestly want Christ to control your life? If not, ask God to change your heart. Thank Him, by faith, that He has begun to do so.

2 List areas of your life that you believe should be brought under the control of Jesus Christ.

3 Ask God to show you ways to bring these areas under His control.

4 To make 1 John 1:9 meaningful in your life:

- ◆ List your sins and failures on a separate sheet of paper.
- ◆ Claim 1 John 1:9 for your own life by writing the words of the verse over the list.
- ◆ Thank God for His forgiveness and cleansing.
- ◆ Destroy the list.
- ◆ Make restitution wherever appropriate and possible.

Five Principles of Growth

❖

Objective: To understand the essentials of Christian growth and put them into practice

Read: James 1:18–27; Matthew 26:31–75; 1 Corinthians 12:12–27; Acts 26:12–29

Memorize: 2 Timothy 2:15

Y ou made the most important decision of your life when you chose to receive Jesus Christ as your Savior and Lord. At that moment you were born into God's family, and you received everything you need to live the abundant Christian life.

But that does not mean you are as spiritually mature as someone who has walked with Christ for many years. The Christian life is a process that begins with an act of faith and is lived by faith.

What do you suppose would happen to a child who doesn't grow properly in his physical body? In his emotional life? In his spiritual maturity? Just as physical life requires air, food, rest, and exercise, so does spiritual life require certain things for growth and development.

This lesson deals with five principles of Christian growth. The first two, *We must study God's Word* and *We must pray,* help us deepen our relationship with God. This could be called our vertical relationship. Through the Bible, God communicates to us; through prayer, we communicate with Him.

The next two principles, *We must fellowship with other Christians* and *We must wit-*

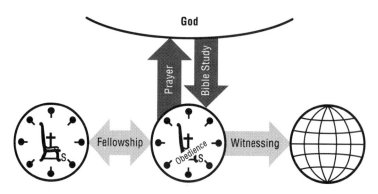

ness for Christ, help us reach out to others. This could be called our horizontal relationship. In fellowship, we communicate with other Christians about our Savior and the bond He gives us with one another. In witnessing, we communicate with non-Christians. We tell them about Jesus, what He has done for us, and what He desires to do for them.

Principle five, *We must obey God,* is the core of the growth. As we obey Him, we experience increasing joy, peace, and fellowship with the Lord Jesus Christ and fellow believers. We also become increasingly more mature in our Christian walk.

If you follow these principles, you can be sure that you will grow toward spiritual maturity in Christ.

❖

Bible Study

Principle One: We Must Study God's Word
Read James 1:18–27.

You would not think of going without physical food for a week or even a day, would you? It is necessary for physical life. Without food, we become weakened and eventually may become ill. Lack of spiritual food produces the same results in our spiritual lives.

1. What is the food of the young Christian (1 Peter 2:2)?

In what ways have you made it a consistent spiritual diet?

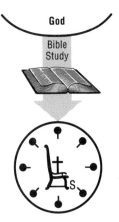

Read Psalm 119. Write down several ways that God's Word can help you in your daily life.

2. Jesus said, "Man shall not live by bread alone." How did He say we should live and be nourished (Matthew 4:4)?

How have you applied this to your life? Describe how it has nourished your spiritual life.

3. List the two characteristics of the workman God approves, according to 2 Timothy 2:15.

1)

2)

What steps have you taken to make these characteristics true in your life?

4. What did Jesus say about those who read and believe God's Word (John 8:31,32)?

What does this mean to your way of life?

5. When does the man who is spiritually mature meditate on the Word of God (Psalm 1:2,3)?

How can you do this in our hectic, pull-apart world?

6. In what specific ways do you expect God's Word to affect you?

Principle Two: We Must Pray

Read Matthew 26:31–75.

Have you ever considered that you have immediate access to the most powerful Person in the universe? Whatever you need, whatever the time, you can call upon Him. His calendar is cleared to be with you; His schedule is open for your appointment; His full attention is devoted to you.

Prayer is the inspiring experience of conversing with and praising God as our loving, heavenly Father. Few experiences can equal prayer in empowering us and

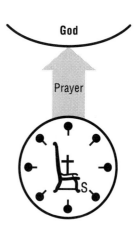

lifting us above our problems. But prayer is not just an "escape hatch" for us to get out of trouble, please ourselves, or gain our selfish ends.

Rather, it is inviting Him to talk to us as we talk to Him. There is more to prayer, but this is basic to true prayer.

Study the above passage and answer the following questions:

1. What was Jesus' command in Matthew 26:41?

Why did He command it?

2. Why did Peter fail to resist temptation?

3. What was the most serious result of Peter's prayerlessness?

Think about your own prayer life. What has been the result of prayerlessness in your life?

4. How did Christ experience inner power to face the severest test of His life?

5. How often are we to pray (1 Thessalonians 5:17)?

Prayer without ceasing involves conversing with our heavenly Father in a simple and free way throughout the day. Our prayer life should be such that we come to know the Lord Jesus in an intimate, personal way. Our prayer life becomes effective as our relationship with Christ becomes more intimate.

> I will do whatever you ask in my name, so that the Son may bring glory to the Father. You may ask me for anything in my name, and I will do it (John 14:13,14).

List ways you can increase the amount of time you spend in prayer.

Principle Three: We Must Fellowship With Other Christians
Read 1 Corinthians 12:12–27.

Fellowship is spending time and doing things with others who love Christ. Several logs burn brightly together, but the fire goes out if one is placed alone on the cold hearth. In the same way, Christians need to work together or the fire of enthusiasm will go out. Fellowship is vital for Christian growth. That is why active participation in church is so important.

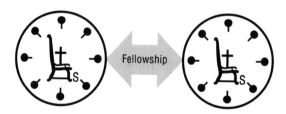

1. As God's children, what should we not neglect (Hebrews 10:23–25)?

2. According to the above verses, what should we do for one another?

In what ways have you done them recently and for whom?

3. The new believers in Acts 2:42 continued steadfastly in what four things?

1)

2)

3)

4)

Why is each one so vital to spiritual growth?

4. In what ways do you profit from Christian fellowship? Be specific.

5. Why is it important that a Christian be part of a small group with other Christians sharing the Word of God?

Why is it so necessary to work out conflicts with members of your Christian circle?

What can happen if you don't?

What steps can you take to resolve conflict with others? (Read 1 Peter 3:8–11.)

Principle Four: We Must Witness for Christ
Read Acts 26:12–29.

A witness is a person who tells what he has seen and heard. He shares his own personal experience. Anyone who has a vital personal relationship with Christ can be a witness for Him. Witnessing is the overflow of the Christian life. A vital Christian life is contagious. As our lives are filled with the presence of the Lord Jesus, we cannot help but share Him with those with whom we come in contact.

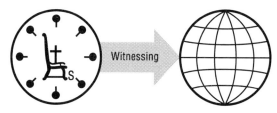

1. In Romans 1:14–16, Paul tells us his own attitude about sharing the gospel with others. Using his three "I am's" as the keys to the passage, describe his attitude in your own words.

2. Compare your own attitude concerning witnessing with Paul's (Colossians 1:28).

3. What did Peter tell us we should always be ready to do (1 Peter 3:15)?

Where and when can you do this?

4. What was Jesus' promise in Acts 1:8?

How is His promise shown in your life today?

5. Name at least three people to whom you are impressed to witness in the power of Christ.

1)

2)

3)

Prayerfully ask God to show you ways to share your faith in Christ with each one.

It is the privilege and responsibility of every Christian to reach his world with the message of Christ. If you would like to receive more information on how to witness effectively for Christ, write to Campus Crusade for Christ, 100 Sunport Lane, Dept. 21-00, Orlando, FL 32809. Ask for specially prepared materials to help you witness for Christ.

Principle Five: We Must Obey God
Read Romans 6:14–23.

The key to rapid growth in the Christian life is obedience to the will of God. Knowing the principles of growth is of no value unless we actually apply them to our lives. To be disobedient to the one who loves us and who alone knows what is really best for us would be sheer folly. Remember, He is even more desirous than you are that you have an abundant life.

1. What did Christ teach concerning the possibility of serving more than one master (Matthew 6:24)?

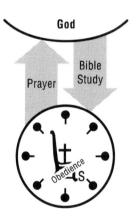

2. How much should you love the Lord (Matthew 22:37)?

3. How can you prove that you love Him (John 14:21)?

How have you done this today?

This week?

4. What will be the result of keeping Christ's commandments (John 15:10,11)?

5. What is God's standard of life for those who say they are abiding in Christ (1 John 2:6)?

6. Where do we get the power to obey God (Philippians 2:13)?

What happens if we try to obey God's commands in our own effort?

7. In light of Luke 6:46–49, why do you think obedience to Christ is imperative for your life?

L I F E   A P P L I C A T I O N

On this chart, list the five key principles of Christian growth, a key verse relating to each one, why it is essential to spiritual maturity, and at least one way you can apply each principle to your own life.

PRINCIPLE	KEY VERSE	WHY IT IS ESSENTIAL	HOW TO APPLY

The Christian's Authority

Before I became a believer in Jesus Christ, God's Word did not make sense to me. I occasionally tried to read it during my high school and college days, but found it boring. Finally, I concluded that no really intelligent person could believe the Bible.

Then I became a Christian.

My life was transformed, and my attitudes concerning the Scriptures changed. I realized the Bible was truly the holy, inspired, and eternally authoritative Word of God.

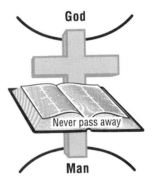

God

Never pass away

Man

Objective: To understand the role and the power of the Bible in our daily Christian lives

Read: Psalm 119:97–104

Memorize: 1 Thessalonians 2:13

Not only is God's Word divinely inspired, but it is also the basis of our belief as Christians. It gives us God's perspective on how we should live and how we can be fruitful witnesses for our Lord Jesus Christ.

The Bible is God's love letter to man. From Genesis to Revelation, it tells of God's great compassion for us and of His desire to fellowship with us.

43

Furthermore, the Bible reveals God's attributes. It tells us that He is holy, sovereign, righteous and just; that He is loving, merciful and kind; that He is gracious, patient and faithful; that He is powerful, wise, and constantly available to His children.

And the more we read and meditate upon His precious Word— and allow His Holy Spirit to control our lives—the more fruitful we become for our Lord. Because God's Word is truth and "sharper than a two-edged sword," it is impregnated with the power of the Holy Spirit to speak to today's world and our own personal needs and circumstances.

Ultimately our views of the authority of the Bible and of the incarnation of Christ are related. In John 10:34–36, for example, Jesus taught that the Old Testament was totally accurate. In Matthew 4:4–7,10, He quoted it as being authoritative.

In addition, He taught His followers that He was speaking God's own words (John 3:34), and that His words would not pass away but would be eternally authoritative (Matthew 24:35).

He even told us that the Holy Spirit would bring to mind what He said so that the disciples would preach and write accurately, not depending upon only memory or human understanding (John 16:12–15).

A high view of inspiration should be related to personal Bible study and meditation. As you study this lesson, I urge you to apply the principles that you will learn about God's inspired Word to your life. Let God speak to you and invite the Holy Spirit to transform you into a joyful and fruitful Christian.

Bible Study

Biblical Claims of Authority

1. What were the attitudes of the following prophets concerning their writings?

Isaiah 43:1–12

Jeremiah 23:1–8

Ezekiel 36:32–38

2. What were the attitudes of the following authors toward other writers of Scripture?
Paul (Romans 3:1,2)

Peter (2 Peter 1:19–21)

The writer of Hebrews (1:1)

3. If these writers had this high regard for Scripture, how should we view the Bible?

What part should God's Word have in our lives and in the way we evaluate and react to circumstances and events?

Purpose of Personal Bible Study

1. Name some practical results of a thorough study of the Word of God (2 Timothy 3:15–17).

What changes have you seen in your life from your study of the Bible?

2. In Acts 20:32, Paul says that the Word of God is able to do what two things?

1)

2)

3. What should be the effect of reading the Bible on your own life (James 1:22–25)?

Think of a difficult circumstance in your life. In what ways is reading and meditating on God's Word helping you cope with the situation?

How are you applying God's Word to your problem?

Preparations for Personal Bible Study

1. Set aside a definite time.

When did Moses meet with God (Exodus 34:2–4)?

When did Christ meet with God (Mark 1:35)?

When is the best time for you?

2. Find a definite place.
Where did Christ pray (Mark 1:35)?

What is the value of being alone?

3. Employ these tools:
   ◆ Modern translation of the Bible
   ◆ Notebook and pen
   ◆ Dictionary
How can you use these tools in your Bible study?

Procedure for Personal Bible Study

Using Psalm 119:57–104, go through these three major steps of methodical Bible study:

   1. *Observation:* What does the passage say? Read quickly for content.
   Read again carefully, underlining key words and phrases.

2. *Interpretation:* What does the passage mean? Ask God to give you understanding of the passage. Consult a dictionary or modern translation for the precise meaning of words.

Ask: Who? What? When? Where? Why? How?

3. *Application:* Ask yourself, *What does the passage mean to me and how can I apply it to my life?*

Make a list of the following:

◆ Attitudes to be changed

◆ Actions to take or avoid

◆ Promises to claim

◆ Sins to confess and forsake

◆ Examples to follow

◆ Other personal applications

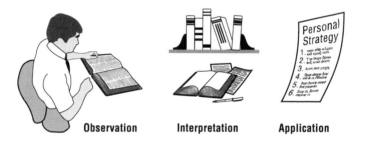

Observation   **Interpretation**   **Application**

LIFE APPLICATION

❶ Study Luke 19:1–10 and apply the Bible study method you have just learned.

What does the passage say?

What does it mean?

How does this apply to you?

How effective will this method of Bible study be for you now with other Scripture passages?

❷ What changes in your life do you expect as you proceed with more in-depth Bible study?

❸ Plan your Bible study time for the next four weeks. Write down the time, the place, and the passages to be studied.

Learning to Pray

Communication is a vital element in any successful relationship, including our relationship with God. He wants us to communicate with Him about our cares and concerns. He desires that we talk to Him about every area of our lives. This communication with God is called prayer.

Prayer is much more than words. It is an expression of the heart toward God. It is an experience, a relationship—not an activity.

As a child of God, you are invited to come boldly before His throne. In Hebrews 4:14–16, the writer records, "Since we have a great High Priest who has gone through the heavens, Jesus the Son of God, let us...then approach the throne of grace with confidence, so that we may receive mercy and find grace to help us in time of need."

Because the one to whom you pray is the King of kings and Lord of lords, the Creator of heaven and earth, you come into His pre-

Objective: To learn how to develop a personal prayer life

Read: Philippians 4:6; Psalm 62:8; Acts 4:23–33

Memorize: Mark 11:24

sence with reverence. But He is also your loving, heavenly Father who cares for you. Therefore, you can enter into His presence with a relaxed, joyful heart, knowing that God loves you more than anyone else has ever loved you or will ever love you.

Bible Study

What Is Prayer?

Since prayer is communication between two persons, it can also be described as a dialogue. Write a sentence about the part each of these have in the dialogue between the believer and God.

1. Prayer is the privilege of believers (John 3:22,23).

2. We relate to God like children to a father (Ephesians 2:4,5,8; 1 Peter 5:7).

3. God wants to hear what we say (Psalms 62:8; 65:2; Proverbs 15:8).

4. God delights in and longs for our fellowship (Psalm 27:8; John 4:23; Proverbs 15:8).

5. We can talk to God about anything (Matthew 7:7; John 16:24).

6. Prayer can keep us from sin (Matthew 26:41).

How to Pray

1. What part does the Holy Spirit play in prayer (Romans 8:26,27)?

2. What do these verses teach about how to pray?
Psalm 145:18

Matthew 6:5–7

Matthew 21:22

Philippians 4:6

3. What vital elements of prayer are found in Acts 4:24–30?

4. What vital elements of prayer did Christ include in His prayer in John 17?

5. What are some of the promises Christ makes to you when you pray?

Matthew 6:6

Matthew 18:20

Luke 11:9–13

John 14:13,14

Steps to Having an Effective Prayer Life

Read the following verses and explain why each step is necessary to pray effectively.

1. Abide (John 15:7)

2. Ask (James 4:2,3)

3. Believe (Matthew 21:22)

4. Receive (1 John 5:14,15)

L I F E   A P P L I C A T I O N

❶ Set a time and place for your daily prayer time.

Time _____   Place _____

❷ Use a small notebook to help you pray effectively.

♦ On page one, make a list of people whom you want to remember daily in prayer.

♦ On page two, write a list of things for which you will praise and thank God. Update this list daily.

♦ On page three, write the date, prayer requests, and Scripture verses relating to requests. Leave room to write down the answer and date for each request.

♦ Each day, repeat the first two points, checking for answered prayers to record on earlier days.

♦ Keep this notebook with your Bible so you can refer to it during the day to pray for and record concerns, needs, praises, or thanks that come to mind.

The Importance of the Church

A young mother once asked her child if he knew what a church was. With a big smile on his face, he said, "Yes, Mommy, that's where God lives."

Of course, the child's perception that God lives in a single, physical place is incorrect. Nevertheless his statement is profound: God does live in the church—the company of all who believe in Jesus Christ and have received Him as their Savior and Lord.

In a broad biblical sense, the church is the body of Christ—the collection of Christian believers from all over the world and from all times who are bound together by the shed blood of Christ and His resurrected presence.

In our local congregations, we play an important part of the body of Christ. God wants us to work together so that the church body can minister to others more effectively.

The church also is a unity of the Holy Spirit. Although doctrinal differences often separate Christian groups, they are united in the fact that Jesus paid the penalty for our sins by dying on the cross, and He rose from the dead that through Him we can be reconciled to God.

❖

Objective: To emphasize the importance of involvement in a local church

Read: Acts 2:41–47

Memorize: Colossians 1:18

The outreach of the church is world-wide. When our Lord's earthly ministry was completed, He commanded the church to carry His good news to the world. By sharing our faith in Christ, we are helping to fulfill this Great Commission.

I am convinced that a proper understanding of the church and how it is to function as a local body is important if we are to be fruitful disciples for Christ.

Some time ago I struck up a conversation with the passenger sitting next to me on a plane flight. As we talked, he was very cordial and pleasant.

Then I asked, "Where are you on your spiritual journey?"

Suddenly, he became defensive. "I had my fill of the church when I was a young boy. Can you believe that I was forced to attend services at least three times a week? Every Sunday morning and evening and every Wednesday night. Years ago I determined that when I became an adult I would never attend church again as long as I live."

"How would you like to live in a community where there was no church?" I inquired.

He dropped his head and was silent for a few moments. Then he replied, "I wouldn't like that."

Looking him firmly in the eye, I said forcefully, "You are a parasite!"

Immediately he became flustered and said impatiently, "What do you mean by that?"

"Simple. You want all the benefits of the church without any of the responsibility."

He smiled slowly, returned my direct gaze, then announced, "For the first time in twenty-five years, I'll be in church on Sunday!"

Before I became a Christian, I used to believe that the church was filled with hypocrites. Now I recognize that many people go to church—not because they are perfect—but because they need help. The church then, in the vernacular of the business world, is a repair shop, not a retail store. The church is not perfect, but it is the institution that offers hope and healing in any community or culture. It is how God reaches out to others with His love and forgiveness.

I urge you to study this lesson prayerfully and carefully. As you continue in your study of the Bible, search out passages that describe the church and its ministry on earth. Keep a diary of your studies for future reference.

Bible Study

Composition of the Church

1. What did the early Christians do that we should do also?
Acts 2:41,42

Acts 4:31

Acts 5:41,42; 8:4

List several ways you can apply these in your Christian walk.

2. As God's children, how do we obey the instruction given in Hebrews 10:25?

3. The entire church is compared to a _____ of which Christ is the _____ and the individual believers are the _____ (Colossians 1;18; 1 Corinthians 12:27).

4. Read 1 Thessalonians 1:1–10, then list here some qualities God desires in members of any church.

In what ways do you demonstrate these qualities?

Ordinances of the Church

1. What do you believe baptism accomplishes (Matthew 28:19)?

Who is eligible for baptism?

What was the significance of your baptism?

2. What is the meaning of the communion service
(1 Corinthians 11:23–26)?

How do you prepare yourself to observe the Lord's Supper?

Purposes of the Church

1. What should be one of the basic purposes of a church
(2 Timothy 4:2)?

How does the church you attend fulfill the purposes given
in this verse?

2. List several of your own reasons for joining a church.

3. What should the church believe about Christ's:
Birth (Matthew 1:23)?

Deity (John 1:14)?

Death (1 Peter 2:24)?

Resurrection (1 Corinthians 15:3,4)?

Second coming (1 Thessalonians 4:16,17)?

Where does your church stand on these truths? It may be
helpful to obtain a doctrinal statement from your church
and research these areas.

4. What abilities does God give (besides that of serving as a
prophet or apostle) to strengthen the church members
(Ephesians 4:11–13)?

Which of these roles do you fill?

Which would you like to be involved in?

Why?

How are you preparing yourself for that ministry?

L I F E   A P P L I C A T I O N

1 If you are not already active in a local church, prayerfully list two or three that you will visit in the next month, with the purpose of attending one regularly.

Before you attend the first service, list the qualities you feel are essential for spiritual growth and fellowship. Ask God to show you which church He is leading you to join.

2 The following are suggestions for making your church worship more meaningful:

♦ Bow for silent prayer before the service begins. Pray for yourself, for the minister, for those taking part in the service and for those worshiping, that Christ will be very real to all, and that those who do not know Christ may come to know Him.

♦ Always take your Bible. Underline portions that are made especially meaningful by the sermons.

♦ Take notes on the sermon and apply them to your life.

Can you list some other ways?

3 If you are a part of a local church, ask God to show you ways you can be more used by Him in the church. List the ways of service that He reveals to you.

Recap

The following questions will help you review this Step. If necessary, reread the appropriate lesson(s).

1. Assurance of salvation:

Suppose you have just made the great discovery of knowing Jesus Christ personally. In your enthusiasm, you tell someone close to you that you have become a Christian and have eternal life. He replies, "That's mere presumption on your part. No one can be sure that he has eternal life."

How would you answer him?

Reread: John 3:1–20; 1 John 5:9–15; Romans 6:14–23

Review: Verses memorized

What verse(s) would you use as your authority?

2. How can a Christian be restored to fellowship after he has sinned?

What Scripture reference is your authority?

3. Name some of the qualities of a Christ-controlled life.

How are they evident in your life?

4. List the five principles of growth.

1)

2)

3)

4)

5)

Summarize briefly how each of these principles are helping you grow spiritually. How do they interact in your life?

5. Describe the role that the Bible has played in your life in the past week.

How can you rely more fully on its power next week?

6. What are the three major steps in methodical Bible study?

1)

2)

3)

How have these helped you in your study?

7. List at least three ways Scripture can be applied to your life.

1)

2)

3)

8. How has using the steps to an effective prayer life changed the way you pray?

9. How has having a daily prayer time helped your attitudes and actions?

10. Name some characteristics of a New Testament church.

How does your church compare?

LIFE APPLICATION

1 In what specific ways is your life different now than when you began this study about the Christian adventure?

2 In what areas do you need to obey the Scripture more?

3 Explain to several Christian friends the excitement you feel about Jesus and how your Christian life is an adventure. Use examples of how God has worked in your life and how He has answered your prayers.

Keys to Dynamic Living
How to Live a Joyful, Fruitful, Spirit-filled Life

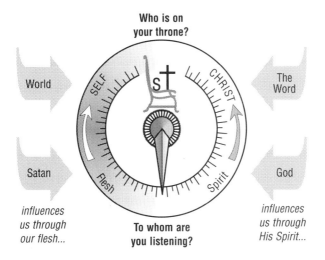

Who is on your throne?

World

The Word

Satan

God

influences us through our flesh...

To whom are you listening?

influences us through His Spirit...

In this diagram, the circle is our life. The chair is the throne of our life, our control center. Both God (through His Spirit) and Satan (through our flesh) desire to control that throne. God wants to bless us with abundant life and fellowship with Himself. Satan wants initially to satisfy our fleshly desires but eventually to destroy us. Positive, uplifting, creative, and beneficial thoughts come to us from God through the Holy Spirit. Self-gratifying, negative, and self-destructive thoughts come to us from Satan through our flesh, our old unregenerate nature (Galatians 5:16–18; Romans 7:15–8:8).

Resisting Temptation
When faced with a tempting thought, ask yourself, "To whom am I listening?" If it is not Christ-honoring, stop immediately and consciously turn the dial of your thoughts (like turning a radio dial for a different program) and pray, "Lord, I am turning the dial of my thoughts toward You. I choose to listen to Your thoughts and surrender the control of the throne of my life to You." Begin to praise

God, read His Word, and—when necessary—talk with a mature Christian friend about the Lord until all traces of that tempting voice have vanished, and you are aware of God's presence directing your thoughts and desires (1 Corinthians 10:13; Philippians 4:4–8).

Spiritual Breathing

Just as in physical breathing as you exhale the impure and inhale the pure, when you sin by committing a deliberate act of disobedience, breathe spiritually to restore the fullness of God's Holy Spirit in your life:

Exhale by Confession

"If we confess our sins, He is faithful and just and will forgive us our sins and purify us from all unrighteousness" (1 John 1:9). True confession involves the following:

1. Acknowledge that your sin or sins (name them specifically) are wrong and grievous to God.

2. Acknowledge that you are already forgiven through Christ's death and the shedding of His blood for your sins.

3. Repent (a change of attitude and action).

4. Make restitution, if needed.

Inhale by Appropriation

Surrender the control of your life to Christ and appropriate (receive) the fullness of the Holy Spirit by faith. Trust that God now directs and empowers you, according to the command of Ephesians 5:18, "be filled with the Spirit," and the promise of 1 John 5:14,15, "if we ask anything according to His will, He hears us. And if we know that He hears us—whatever we ask—we know that we have what we asked of Him."

Keys to Dynamic Living is available in a laminated 3×5 card for easy personal reference. Tuck in your pocket, purse, or Bible. Excellent for follow-up of new Christians. Give to your Sunday school class or members of your family and friends.

Resources to Help You Grow in Christ

Ten Basic Steps. A comprehensive curriculum for the Christian who wants to master the basics of Christian growth. Used by hundreds of thousands worldwide. (See page 74 for details.)

The Ten Basic Steps Leader's Guide. Contains Bible study outlines for teaching the complete series.

The Handbook for Christian Maturity. Combines the entire series of the *Ten Basic Steps* in one volume. A handy resource for private Bible study; an excellent book to help nurture spiritual growth and maturity.

Life Without Equal. A presentation of the length and breadth of the Christian's freedom in Jesus Christ and how believers can release Christ's resurrection power for life and ministry. Good for unbelievers or Christians who want to grow in their Christian life.

A Great Adventure. How to become a Christian in the form of a personal letter. Formerly *The Van Dusen Letter*, this tool has helped millions of people find faith in Jesus Christ.

The Holy Spirit: Key to Supernatural Living. This book helps you enter into the Spirit-filled life and shares how you can experience a life of supernatural power and victory.

Keys to Dynamic Living card. Experience a joyful, fruitful, Spirit-filled life and deal with temptation through "spiritual breathing." Small enough to tuck into your pocket, purse, or Bible.

Available through your local Christian bookstore, mail-order catalog distributor, or NewLife Publications.

Ten Basic Steps Toward Christian Maturity

*Eleven easy-to-use individual guides to help you understand
the basics of the Christian faith*

A Time-Tested Study Series Featuring:

INTRODUCTION: The Uniqueness of Jesus
Explains who Jesus Christ is, His earthly life, His death and resurrection, and His
continuing ministry in the lives of all believers. Reveals the secret of His power to turn
you into a victorious, fruitful Christian.

STEP 1: The Christian Adventure
Shows you how to enjoy what millions of other Christians around the world have
experienced—the adventure of a full, abundant, purposeful, and fruitful life in Christ.

STEP 2: The Christian and the Abundant Life
Explores the Christian way of life—what it is and how it works practically. Discusses
the problems of temptation, sin, and spiritual warfare. Points the way to victorious
living.

STEP 3: The Christian and the Holy Spirit
Teaches who the Holy Spirit is, how to be filled with the Spirit, and how to make the
Spirit-filled life a moment-by-moment reality in your life. The truths you learn will
ignite your spirit.

STEP 4: The Christian and Prayer
Shows how to fellowship with God and receive His answers to your prayers. Reveals the
true purpose of prayer and shows how the Father, Son and Holy Spirit work together to
answer your prayers. You will discover how to use the great power of prayer effectively.

STEP 5: The Christian and the Bible
Talks about the Bible—how we got it, its authority, and its power to help the believer.
Offers methods for studying the Bible more effectively. Shows how to claim God's
promises to you as a believer.

STEP 6: The Christian and Obedience

Learn why it is so important to obey God and how to live daily in His grace. Discover the secret to personal purity and power as a Christian and why you need not fear what others think of you.

STEP 7: The Christian and Witnessing

Shows you how to witness effectively in the power of the Holy Spirit and how to know when He is leading you in sharing your faith. Includes a reproduction of the *Four Spiritual Laws* and explains how to share them. Follow the proven concepts of this Step and you will develop confidence to share Christ as a way of life.

STEP 8: The Christian and Giving

Offers sound biblical principles for giving that will enable you to enjoy the promised blessings of God in your life. Discover God's plan for your financial life, how to stop worrying about money, and how to trust God for your finances.

STEP 9: Exploring the Old Testament

Features a brief survey of the Old Testament, including key events, concepts and characters. Shows what God did to prepare the way for Jesus Christ and the redemption of all who receive Him as Savior and Lord. Reveals God's pattern of promise and blessing and explores the true significance of God's grace and forgiveness.

STEP 10: Exploring the New Testament

Reviews each of the New Testament books and contains a brief survey of their contents. Shows the essence of the gospel and highlights the exciting beginning of the Christian church.

Leader's Guide

The ultimate resource for even the most inexperienced, timid and fearful person asked to lead a group study in the basics of the Christian life. No more fumbling for answers. Contains insets revealing both questions and answers from the *Ten Step Study Guides*.

A Handbook for Christian Maturity

Combines the eleven-booklet series into one practical, easy-to-follow volume. Excellent for personal or group study.

Available through your local Christian bookstore, mail-order catalog distributor, or NewLife Publications.

Notes

Notes

Notes

Notes

About the Author

BILL BRIGHT is founder and president of Campus Crusade for Christ International. Serving in 152 major countries representing 98 percent of the world's population, he and his dedicated associates of nearly 50,000 full-time staff, associate staff, and trained volunteers have introduced tens of millions of people to Jesus Christ, discipling millions to live Spirit-filled, fruitful lives of purpose and power for the glory of God.

Dr. Bright did graduate study at Princeton and Fuller Theological seminaries from 1946 to 1951. The recipient of many national and international awards, including five honorary doctorates, he is the author of numerous books and publications committed to helping fulfill the Great Commission. His special focus is New Life 2000, an international effort to help reach more than six billion people with the gospel of our Lord Jesus Christ and help fulfill the Great Commission by the year 2000.